HOW TO BE A
CONVERSATIONAL
SUCCESS!

2ND EDITION

LAURIE SMALE

**HOW TO START A CONVERSATION, KEEP IT GOING,
AND LEAVE A POSITIVE IMPRESSION EVERY TIME**

T0360005

Contents

Acknowledgements

I was recently asked which motivational speakers have influenced me most. My response was immediate. I draw my greatest inspiration from the ordinary people of life's passing parade. For their stories and their contributions have encouraged me to develop and practise my philosophy of panic-free speaking. And to all these people, too numerous to mention, I convey my heartfelt thanks.

I am extremely grateful to and want to acknowledge Winston Marsh, Patricia Cameron-Hill and Shayne Yates for their valued comments on the general feel of this book.

Malcolm Gray, Eva Light and Madalen Ross are also worthy of profound acknowledgement for their timely insights that helped keep me to the point.

Finally, thank you to my meticulous editor, Charlotte Duff, who helped me fine-tune my thoughts, and the rest of the team at Publish Central for their unsurpassed publishing expertise in helping me bring this book to life.

Conversational effectiveness: A big factor in your success

Make no mistake: no matter what your experience or station in life, being an effective – or ineffective – conversationalist can be a deciding factor in your social and business success. Even in this electronic world of social media and communicating by electronic devices, we can't escape the fact that interacting with other human beings face to face remains part of our very existence. Conversation is our principle means of communicating with one another from the moment we get up in the morning until we go to bed at night. Yet, many of us believe that we are less than skilful when it comes to conversation effectiveness.

Why then do some people come across as more spontaneous, interesting and effective human beings when communicating with each other? What's the secret of their conversational success? Are they endowed with some exclusive gift?

SIMPLE PRINCIPLES AND TECHNIQUES FOR CONVERSATIONAL AWARENESS AND UNDERSTANDING

Actually, there are a few simple secrets. These individuals have learned some easy-to-use principles and techniques for starting a conversation, guiding it, and keeping it pleasant and interesting. You can learn these principles easily too. With practice, you'll soon be the confident conversational success you desire to be.

Before looking at how to put these simple techniques into practice, you need to deal with any inner obstacles that might be holding you back. Only then will you be free to enjoy all the social and business benefits that pleasant, agreeable conversation has to offer. This book begins by identifying the basic principles of conversational awareness and understanding, before moving on to the techniques.

HOW TO GET THE MOST OUT OF THIS BOOK

Read this book in sequence to really reap its benefits.

Over a lifetime of developing these ideas, I've come to realise that techniques and skills alone are not the answer. You must first create a solid confidence within yourself upon which to build. This book is divided into two parts for this very important reason: to shift your thinking in a permanent way on who you are and what you stand for before you move on to the commonsense practicalities of everyday conversation. Therefore, to derive the maximum benefit in pleasure and social or business success from these pages, concentrate first on the chapters in part I.

The principles outlined in these chapters are designed to help you recognise you have something to say, widen your conversational horizons, and give you the required self-confidence.

Part II then takes you through eight simple steps to conversational success, including how to start a conversation, keep it going, and close it in a positive way. You will likely readily identify with these steps because they are based on creative commonsense. As your self-imposed constraints and limitations fall away, you'll take ownership of these steps and put them to use immediately. The results will astound you.

By the end of this book, you'll be well on the way to being the confident, intuitive conversationalist you've always wanted to be.

Enjoy the journey.

PART I

Getting YOU right first: The principles of conversation

*In order to succeed,
we must first believe that we can.*

MICHAEL KORDA

CHAPTER 1

The first principle:
To be interesting, be interested

A member of my audience once asked, 'But is it really that easy? Aren't some people born with a natural flair, the "gift of the gab"?'

And I said, 'Sure they are, but so are you – in your own way.'

So let's lay this myth of the 'gifted conversational few' to rest right here. Anyone can be a sparkling conversationalist when they know how. The fact is you are what you think. If you see yourself as a conversational failure, you'll most certainly live up to it. Perception is reality. This book helps you establish a positive view of yourself with regard to your conversational effectiveness – for success builds on success.

SPEAK IN TERMS OF THE OTHER PERSON'S INTERESTS

The financial manager of a large manufacturing firm bitterly complained to me that whenever he had to speak with workers on the shop floor he was defeated before he began. 'They see me as the company "bean counter", stuck away in my office and only interested in balancing the books.'

I said, 'What really matters is how you see yourself. Have you ever spent time among these people to make yourself accessible and understand your facts and figures from their point of view? Do you package what you have to say in immediate examples of real people from the shop floor that relate to them and their experiences? Do you speak in terms of their interests and benefits to them? And, above all, do you ever spend a moment or two enquiring after things that interest them outside of work?'

David admitted he had done precious few of these things. His focus had been 100 per cent on himself, his own perceived shortcomings, and how the all-important figures were travelling. These people were the enemy and the less time spent with them the better. But he soon realised that no-one was out to get him, and that very day he started working on giving himself a new reputation to live up to – one of warmth, helpfulness and accessibility. He rang me three weeks later and said this new approach had worked like magic.

So if we want others to be interested in what we have to say, we must first put to one side our wants and desires and become genuinely interested in them.

BE CONSIDERATE AND NICE TO PEOPLE

When we relate with people, we sell our ideas, our services and our products. But most of all, we sell ourselves. In fact, I'd go as far as saying that most business and social relationships, in some way or another, begin over a friendly chat. Max Hitchins, former National President of the National Speakers Association of Australia (now Professional Speakers Australia), would certainly go along with this.

As a young man fresh from the country, he once found himself out of his depth and standing alone among a group of very influential people. Nervously Max thought, *I wish someone would come and talk to me.*

To his amazement, the most important person of the gathering unobtrusively extricated himself from the people he was talking to and made his way over to Max. He warmly thanked Max for coming and talked in terms of his interests. He made this young lad from the country feel important and influential too! Max has never forgotten this kind and thoughtful gesture.

Unexpected outcome

Years later, Max again found himself among a group of influential business people, only this time he was one of them. During the course of conversation, he spied a man standing to the side by himself. Remembering the kindness afforded him all those years before, he made his way over to him with the sole purpose of being friendly and agreeable and making this person feel welcome.

The guy turned out to be a very influential convention convenor based in Switzerland! He was particularly impressed with the phenomenally successful marketing strategy of Max's perennial book, *Fact, Fiction and Fables of the Melbourne Cup*. Two months later, he booked Max as a keynote conference speaker in Switzerland and, of all places, Iceland!

As a result, Max is now a recognised international speaker on marketing. You see, you never know the outcomes of being just plain considerate and nice to people. It not only creates friendship, but also makes good business sense.

IN A NUTSHELL

- Focus your interest and energy on others instead of your perceived shortcomings.

- Speak in terms of the other person's interests.

- See yourself as a warm, accessible human being.

- If you see someone standing alone at a gathering, pluck up the courage to go and talk to them. You'll both be the richer for it.

CHAPTER 2

The second principle:
See yourself as an expert

In my personal coaching sessions, it's amazing how many people say, 'I've never really done anything exceptional in my life. I'm just a housewife, a technician, a supervisor, a secretary, a teacher, a student, a mental health worker, a bulldozer operator (and so on)'. It's always someone else who is the expert and gets the pat on the back.

Never have they stopped to take stock of their lives and pin down what they've earned the right to feel like an expert in – even if it's in what not to do!

With conversational effectiveness in mind, let's accept the definition of an expert as someone who has earned the right to have something to say through some sort of experience, time and effort.

DISCARD YOUR BLINKERS

The managing director of one of Australia's foremost companies in the supply, installation and servicing of industrial air-conditioning saw himself as little more than a glorified plumber for more than 20 years. 'I started by sweeping the factory floor as a 15-year-old and worked my way up from there.'

Yet in one single day under my guidance, Peter at last saw what others had seen in him for years. He took stock of where he'd been, his remarkable achievements, and the deep respect he'd gained throughout the building industry as a leading authority in his field. He no longer continually puts himself down. He now walks tall with the quiet conviction of someone who has truly earned the right to be an expert.

> *No-one can make you feel inferior*
> *without your consent.*
>
> Eleanor Roosevelt

Likewise with Sandy, a devoted kindergarten teacher for more than 20 years who felt completely at home with her young charges, yet was painfully self-conscious when it came to communicating with adults she didn't know. When asked what she did for a living, she'd hesitate and softly reply, 'I'm just a kindergarten teacher.'

This self-effacing response stirred my passions – for kindergarten teaching is one of the most underrated vocations there is. I told her that, as a father of three children, all of whom went to kindergarten, I understood the devotion and care that go into kindergarten programs. I understood the confidence and social skills that are instilled into these impressionable little people at this time in their lives. So much so, they can't wait to go to primary school! Kindergarten teachers? I'll sing their praises any day!

Sandy 'twigged' that the only person on earth who could hold her head up high with justified pride was herself. Within the space of six weeks, she had started a series of community craft workshops for adults. She soon learned that friendly conversation with strangers was a cinch. All she had to do was transfer what she had been doing successfully for years with her pre-schoolers to this new grown-up situation and simply pitch it at a higher level.

Sandy no longer degrades herself. She now walks tall with a quiet confidence. Her focus now is on how she can help others instead of worrying about her perceived inadequacies.

Her new approach is not unlike the woman I once found myself in pleasant conversation with on a social occasion – a well-dressed professional and very sure of herself. When I asked, 'And what do you do with your time?', her response was telling.

'My chosen career has been managing a household and bringing up three teenage children – of which I'm very proud.' I was momentarily taken aback because I'd assumed something entirely different. She'd obviously sorted herself out long ago and took pride in everything she did. She was an expert in this field.

GET A REAL SENSE OF YOUR WORTHINESS

To help you encapsulate your situation in a positive response too, try a marvellous little technique I first heard from Winston Marsh, one of Australia's foremost business consultants. When someone asks you what you do with your time, don't sell yourself short. Instead, encourage questions and comments with an off-pat response that hints at what you do in an interesting way.

During a friendly conversation, I once asked a young woman what she did for a living. She shrugged. 'Oh, I'm just a systems analyst.'

'And what sort of work do you actually do?' My interest was genuine.

'I help manage one of Australia Post's largest databases.' Wow! If only she'd responded with these words the first time round. This response paints a very different picture compared with her first belittling response of 'just' being a systems analyst. The second response (which should become her off-pat response) conveys a real sense of her own self-worth, and I'm certainly curious to learn more.

NOURISH YOUR SELF-ESTEEM

Here are some more off-pat response examples that engender self-worth and stimulate interest:

- Instead of the factual but uninspiring, 'I'm a librarian', say, 'I'm an information specialist.'
- Instead of the mundane, 'I stack supermarket shelves', nourish your self-esteem with, 'I manage supermarket shelf space.'

The author Ricardo Semler's analogy of the stone cutters working beside the road says it all. One was asked, 'What are you doing?' With eyes cast down, he replied in a flat voice, 'I'm cutting stone.'

In answer to the same question, another stone cutter put his tools down, straightened up and looked the person in the eye and said, 'I'm building a cathedral!'

So whether you're managing a household or running an airline, make sure you see yourself as a cathedral builder.

> *We ask ourselves, 'Who am I to be*
> *brilliant, gorgeous, talented, fabulous?'*
> *Actually, who are you not to be?*
>
> Marianne Williamson

RESPOND WITH SOMETHING POSITIVE

Even if you're looking for a job, respond with something positive! A response like, 'Up until recently I've been successfully involved in sales … right now I'm in between opportunities', will do a lot more to create rapport and stimulate pleasant conversation than the dreary, self-defeating, 'I'm unemployed.'

If the title of your work tends to paint a negative picture, leave the title out of your prepared response. For example, a young chap recently told me, 'I work with animals.' I immediately saw him as a zookeeper or some sort of animal trainer. But I soon learned that he was a butcher! We both had a good laugh and moved on with the conversation. A woman told me that she helped people get their lives back on track after they split up. She turned out to be a family lawyer.

At other times, a job can be deemed 'lowly' by society. After falling into conversation with a chap on a social occasion, he happened to mention that he was a concrete sculptor. Intrigued, I asked him exactly what it was that he sculpted and if he had his own gallery where he exhibited his works. 'I fashion driveways,' he said with pride. 'They're works of art and will be used and admired for a long time.' He had it right and carried himself with the self-assurance of a clever artist. His response was much better than living with the supposedly lowly tag of 'concrete worker'.

Before you read on, take time out to prepare an off-pat response to just what it is you do with your time. Be creative. Make sure it hints at – or spells out – the nature of your job or pastime. And make sure it's positive! This prepared response will not only give you a real sense of your own worthiness, but also help break the ice, generate interest and pave the way for friendly, enjoyable conversation.

COMPARE YOURSELF TO YOUR OWN POTENTIAL

In one of my coaching sessions, a young woman fresh out of university said she felt totally overwhelmed by the collective knowledge, experience and successes of her highly esteemed scientific colleagues. She'd made the fatal mistake we've all made at some stage of our lives of comparing herself to the abilities and successes of others instead of comparing herself to her own potential. As a consequence, when it came to conversation she felt way out of her depth and simply avoided it.

Sure, Mary did not yet have her colleagues' status, knowledge and experience. But so what?! What she did have was the eagerness to learn and her own experiences as a student. We discovered that Mary already had many highlights and 'learning' experiences that singularly gave her the status of an authority on a number of things.

Recognising your accumulated expertise

Among the many examples of Mary's experiences were the following:

- She'd had a difficult upbringing that required many sacrifices in order to survive her education. In spite of this, she achieved the highest possible grades in her field of micro-technology and spent six months in South Korea as an exchange student.

- Her 12 years in an all-girls school had left her with very definite views on the influence this had on her social skills when it came to dealing with the opposite sex.

- She was once lost in the Victorian Alps and had to survive two nights of subzero temperatures before she was rescued.

And on it went ...

The realisation that she had already 'learned' much and had achieved many notable things in her own right did wonders for Mary's self-esteem. She now accepts herself for what she is and no longer sees herself as a wilting violet when in the company of her exalted colleagues. She is now inspired to ask them questions and learn, instead of being overwhelmed by their presence.

Do what you can, with what you have, where you are.

Quoted by Theodore Roosevelt
in his autobiography

START WITH YOURSELF

A young cabinetmaker once said to me, 'But what if you don't like who you are and you don't like where you've been?' This momentarily threw me. Through his eyes, his life had been one disaster after another with nothing to be proud of. His hitherto successful carpentry business had collapsed. His marriage was a dismal failure. And to cap it all off, people had laughed at him when he misjudged a bend and rode his bike headlong into a duck pond. This was the last straw.

He quickly sold his house and moved to Victoria in search of happiness and peace of mind. But he soon learned that you can't 'run anywhere' to discover these precious things. Happiness and peace of mind must start with self-acceptance – after all, we all experience disasters and successes of one kind or another in our lives. He now acknowledges that he has his own bank of accumulated expertise from which to draw. He no longer avoids people or hangs his head in shame when communicating with others for he realises he has something to contribute. Most important of all, he now realises he can't change life's journey. He now likes who he is and learns from where he's been.

The point here is this: it's so easy to belittle ourselves by falling for the trap of comparing ourselves to others and then deciding we don't measure up to their life successes. How do you know their background story and the painful trials they might have endured to be where they are? We can always find people greater and lesser than ourselves. What's important is learning from everyone you meet and moving forward enriched in some way. And the real secret is to compare ourselves to our own potential and not the status and accomplishments of others.

I remember how I felt as a 17-year-old budding professional cyclist. All my friends were at the start to see me off at my first road race, and I was riding my brand new road bike with Campagnolo gears! I felt indestructible and was bursting with enthusiasm, yet it turned into a complete disaster. At first, I felt on top of the world. However, 20 kilometres into the 140-kilometre race my legs turned to lead and the back bunch of seasoned professionals surged past me as if I were standing still.

Totally humiliated, I struggled on through the wind and rain for hours till I arrived at the finish line in darkness. Everyone had gone home for they thought I had been picked up by a support vehicle. Exhausted, I remember toppling over into the mud beside the road and crying. *How will I ever compare to how good those top cyclists are?* I lamented as I lay strapped into my toe clips. Then, with nowhere else to go I slowly dragged myself up and got back on my bike.

As I slowly rode the 20 kilometres home, it began to dawn on me that to reach the status of those topnotch riders who had so thoroughly trounced me, I needed to start from where I was and slowly work my way up towards where they were. And that's exactly what I did, with smaller gains leading to bigger accomplishments. Two years later, I proudly won the A-Grade Champion sash of the Mornington Cycling Club.

Now I was one of the 'big boys' in my *own right* and in my *own way*. This experience taught me the invaluable lesson that comparing ourselves to others in a belittling way can have the negative affect of holding us back from expanding our potential for years. Hard-learned insights such as these are great to toss into a conversation in the right time and the right place to keep the conversation going. (You'll learn more about this in chapter 9.)

Be confident.

Too many days are wasted comparing ourselves to others and wishing to be something we aren't

Everybody has their own strengths and weaknesses, and it is only when you accept, everything you are and everything you aren't that you will truly succeed in life.

Ritu Ghatourey

DRAW FROM YOUR WELL OF WISDOM

So a moment's thought will confirm that you, and you alone, are the only person who can talk with personal conviction on your journey. Here's how to come to terms with the fact that you are indeed clever and have earned the right to be an authority on several things.

Take some time out and reflect on the trials, tribulations and exciting things you've done with your life. Where else can your point of view on a given issue stem from but from your life experiences? Where else can you discover what you stand for?

These are the authentic sources of your fundamental values and convictions, which of course go on changing as you change.

Remember – you don't have to have a PhD to be an authority on something. You may even be a highly qualified expert on how *not* to do it! Keep a record of these things. As each happening or experience comes to mind, encapsulate it in a single sentence. This sentence could signal a five-minute incident or a ten-year haul. Similar to looking at photos, a glance at one of these mental joggers will allow you to revisit a given experience whenever you wish. The single phrase, 'Lost in the Alps', would instantly have our earlier example of Mary reliving her ordeal and how she was saved. The title, 'Round the bend and in the drink', would enable our cabinetmaker friend, with the wisdom of hindsight, to see the funny side of his humiliating headlong dive into the duck pond.

I keep a simple exercise book with about 50 of these gems in a timeline sequence from my earliest memory, to which I'm adding all the time. I continually draw great strength and insight from them.

You could take this list one step further by using it as a wonderful template to write your own autobiography.

Here are some examples of what to note down to get your mind working:

- The trials and tribulations you have experienced to gain recognition or special achievement
- Your earliest memory
- A tale of the unexpected
- Your first job

- A tragedy you experienced or personal fear you overcame
- Your experience as a young immigrant to Australia

The list could go on, but hopefully you get the idea.

With this mini-autobiography, you have now identified your own well of wisdom and self-esteem purely for the positive nourishment of your own thinking. This is where you must first believe in yourself as a true expert on things you may have previously deemed irrelevant and unimportant. And, just as important, this priceless well of experience will provide you with a clear understanding of what's necessary to express an informed opinion.

You are now ready to take the next step: formulating something definite to say.

IN A NUTSHELL

- Take stock of your 'lessons' and achievements and acknowledge your right to consider yourself an expert.

- Accept yourself as an authority on something. You'll walk tall with the quiet confidence of 'having been there'.

- Start your own list of 'learnings' and achievements – reflect on them often.

- When someone asks you, 'What do you do with your time?', stimulate conversation with an off-pat response that spells out or hints at what you do in an interesting way.

- Compare yourself to your own potential, rather than the abilities and achievements of others.

- Become aware of yourself and your own achievements, and you'll become aware of others and theirs.

CHAPTER 3

The third principle: Delineate your point of view

For the first 30 years of my life, I often felt like a fish out of water and found it very difficult to express an opinion on anything of substance when cornered into a conversation.

Having left school at 13 because I couldn't fathom arithmetic, I spent the next 24 years struggling with the awful stigma of mathematical illiteracy and my fear of not having a proper education. At 37, I decided to stop running and do something about this paranoia that was ruining my life. I went back to full-time school, and six years later ended up with my Bachelor of Arts and Diploma in Education, majoring in Australian History and Italian.

Apart from my degree, of which I'm very proud, the two main things I received from my studies are the ability to think clearly and the confidence to express an opinion on a given subject – whether gained through study or my own experiences. I no longer look on my past as something to be ashamed of. On the contrary, I know I also have my very own bank of human interest from which to draw. If only I'd known, I could have drawn inspiration for definite things to say from this bank years ago.

> *Make the most of who you are …*
> *for that is all there is of you.*
>
> Ralph Waldo Emerson

EARNING THE RIGHT TO AN OPINION

Based on my experiences, I feel I've earned the right to have an informed opinion on the following subjects:

- How easy it is to accept oneself as a hapless victim of circumstance and do nothing about it.
- Growing up in a country environment.
- What it's like to hide in 'lowly' jobs because you fear mathematics.
- The incredible insights to be gained from learning a second language.
- How to successfully manage camping tours around Europe and Central Australia.
- The apprehension of going back to school with students half your age.
- The challenges of bringing up a family.
- Overcoming the fear of speaking in public.
- How to face up to and conquer our greatest fears.

Authority and conviction

The point is this: no-one likes a shallow know-all. To have an opinion about anything of substance, you must first earn the right. And where else can you speak with more authority and conviction than from your never-ending experiences? They are the central source of your core values and beliefs, which, as mentioned earlier, are themselves subject to change. It makes no difference how old you are, what your level of education, or how insignificant you perceive your example to be.

When you speak from the heart, you will always have something definite and interesting to contribute.

Think of the many intriguing, and sometimes painful, paths you have trodden in your life. Believe me – you've earned the right to have an opinion on every one of them!

Who you are and what you stand for

Now I'm not advocating you collar everyone you meet and hit them with your life story. The purpose of this book so far has been to permanently shift your thinking so you know you are not an empty vessel, to help you identify a personal source of self-esteem, and to nourish a quiet confidence within you. This will help others get a sense that you know who you are and the things you stand for.

In the chapters in part II, you'll learn eight simple steps that will show you how to build on and transfer this confidence to a wider range of opinions and definite things to say. But first, let's extend your conversational effectiveness by looking beyond yourself to the common connections you have with other people ...

IN A NUTSHELL

- When you speak from your own experience, your words ring true.

- You have earned the right to have an opinion on every experience, every path you've trodden in your life.

- Reflect on your experiences, both good and bad. They are your personal source of wisdom and self-esteem.

- Take courage. Toss a relevant comment into the conversation and see what happens!

- Build on your conviction and experiences; nourish a quiet confidence within.

CHAPTER 4

The fourth principle: Every person you meet is a fascinating package of human interest

We've already established the fact that each of us has a fascinating story to tell. Yet sadly, many people see their lives as uninteresting, run-of-the-mill affairs of little interest to anybody. They actually tell me, 'My life's pretty ordinary ... I've never really done anything outstanding.'

AN AMAZING STORY

Irena felt this way. She saw herself as nothing exceptional. She was just another person striving to make her way in life and give her family the best she possibly could. A sincere interest and a few questions, however, tapped into an amazing story.

Part of a family of eight, Irena well remembers the political upheaval when the Ayatollah Khomeini came to power in her native Iran. 'From one day to the next, my opportunities and movements were restricted.' Whenever she ventured outdoors, she was compelled to cover herself from head to toe with the reintroduced traditional dress discarded decades before. Failure to comply meant instant prison – or worse.

What's more, she was a Christian in mainly Islamic Iran, which at the time was a genuine concern. Finally, she could take it no longer and decided to make her escape.

Unimaginable terror

In the dead of night, she and an accomplice gathered her two little boys and a few meagre belongings and made a run for it across the Iranian desert in a four-wheel drive army vehicle.

After a harrowing journey of unimaginable terror, they finally made it to Australia. They then needed to overcome the formidable cultural and language barriers in order to make this strange new land their home.

Now who wouldn't be interested in that?

All of us like to hear about the trials and tribulations of other human beings, and we like to share our experiences with them. And this is the real essence of conversational success. Your story is my story, and my story is your story. In one way or another, we've all crossed that desert. We're all travelling the same journey.

DON'T JUMP TO CONCLUSIONS

Like most of us, I've often fallen victim to the curse of assumption. Some time back, I had an hour to kill before an important interview and decided to go for a walk along the pier to mull over my approach. It was a cold and windy day, my only companion an old drunkard at the end of the pier fishing with a line wound round a coke bottle.

As I neared him, the devastating effects of alcohol were all too evident. His gnarled hands were blue and almost useless as he rummaged around in an old plastic bucket. His face had a similar hue. *What a life!* I thought to myself. *What a miserable lonely life!* I felt sorry for him.

Warm and friendly

My walk finished, I was about to get into my car when my forsaken companion shuffled by. 'Did you catch anything?' I enquired.

He put his bucket down near a battered old Valiant. 'Nah, too windy. They won't bite when there's an Easterly.' His voice was warm and friendly, and invited more conversation.

In spite of the biting wind and the heavy mist that was now falling, we spent the next half-hour engrossed in fascinating conversation. Contrary to my initial impressions, he was not suffering from alcoholism. He had contracted asbestosis as a result of many years in the building industry. Fishing was one of his greatest joys and the thrill of the chase helped keep his mind off his predicament. The coke bottle was easier to handle than an intricate rod and reel.

I was flabbergasted to learn that he owned a multimillion-dollar building company and had constructed four of Melbourne's largest motel complexes – one of which I was about to have my appointment in! He had travelled the world and was widely read. He literally beamed when he told of his son who had recently set up a business servicing North Sea oil rigs off the coast of Norway. You can imagine how guilty I felt as all this unfolded!

That half-hour conversation, in a cold and windswept car park, did both of us a world of good.

As I drove away, I vowed never to make judgements about people from a distance again. I now try to clear my mind of all negative impressions to make way for a friendly, agreeable interaction with everyone I meet.

> *There's a story behind every person.*
> *There's a reason why they're the way they are.*
> *Think about that before you judge someone.*
>
> An unknown (and wise) person

CONNECTING WITH PEOPLE

What is important here is the absolute certainty that every single person you'll ever meet is a walking, talking package of human interest. Effective conversation, therefore, doesn't come from being endowed with some wonderful communicating gift from on high, or grappling with the 'right' words. The engaging conversationalist simply connects with the other person's passions and interests. It's all about empathy and looking for similarities. It's all about stepping into their experiences, seeking to understand, and giving them the time of day. Occasionally, we stumble across someone who shares our passions too – and that's a bonus!

This insightful knowledge that everyone's experiences are just lying there waiting to be 'triggered' prompts the question: now that you've got yourself right and have a wider understanding of what makes you tick, what specific techniques do you use to feel at ease with people you don't know and get a conversation going? The eight simple steps to conversational success in part II will show you how.

IN A NUTSHELL

- The so-called trivialities of life are the things that make us all tick.

- In one way or another, we're all travelling the same journey.

- Encourage the other person to talk about their interests and tell their story and you'll never run out of things to say.

- Don't jump to conclusions. Clear your mind of all negative thoughts to make way for friendly, agreeable conversation.

PART II

Eight practical steps to conversational effectiveness

Our aspirations are our possibilities.

ROBERT BROWNING

CHAPTER 5

Step 1:
Collect and digest ideas

CULTIVATE A THIRST FOR KNOWLEDGE

Keep your eyes and ears open for interesting tidbits of human interest to add to your own experiences. Become curious and enthusiastic about the world around you and make connections with what you've experienced or what you've read. For example, I recently watched my brother-in-law completely rebuild my two-stroke lawnmower.

It was fascinating. My eagerness to learn had Tony enthusiastically explaining the function of each part and the reason for each step. I've never much been taken by the mechanical side of things, but that day certainly extended my knowledge of what makes a petrol-driven contraption go.

The next time the topic of 'lawnmowers', 'combustion engines', 'leaking oil seals', or even 'storing bits and pieces in marked plastic bags' pops up, I'll have something relevant to toss into the conversation.

WIDEN YOUR HORIZONS

The good conversationalist goes out of their way to keep abreast of things and widen their horizons – unlike the young postal clerk who couldn't work out why he felt so uncomfortable with nothing to say when in a crowd. 'I just clam up when I see everyone else speaking so freely,' he told me. 'If only I had something to say!'

'Do you read much?' I enquired.

'Not really.'

'What about the news? Do you listen to that at least once a day?'

Again his answer was no.

'And what about watching the occasional documentary?'

Now he was feeling uncomfortable: 'No.'

'And when you watch a movie, do you give any thought to its historical context, the story behind it, and its relation to today's world?'

'I've never really thought like that,' he said.

He'd pretty well gone about his life focused on his job and nothing else. If confronted with topics outside this narrow world, he was lost.

I then explained that in order to have something to say, we've got to be active in putting information in our head to draw on.

By listening to or reading about the news at least once a day, we keep up with what's going on in the world. And documentaries further broaden our knowledge of the world we live in. Movies can tell us a lot about ourselves and why we think and act the way we do. These rich sources of information furnish us with definite things to say. And we don't have to remember all these things once we've collected and digested them, for they then just 'come out' when triggered by what the other person is saying.

As for reading, I got him to commit to reading one article every day or so. I particularly like *Reader's Digest*, where each article is only a couple of pages long but is packed with all sorts of human interest and written in a conversational manner – just perfect for finding snippets of relevant interest to toss into a conversation. Of course, *Reader's Digest* isn't the only option you have when looking for good articles. Find what works for you, but try not to rely on simply scrolling through social media and only gaining superficial knowledge from sometimes divisive and less than reputable sources.

Another important tip is to follow your curiosity. Don't wonder *why* something *is* – find out! Search online and find out more about the topic. For example, the other day I wondered why killer whales' teeth were large and round, and not razor-sharp like sharks' teeth. A quick online search told me that they don't need to be sharp because they have immense 'crushing' power. In the right time and right place, this piece of info will come in handy in a conversation.

In the case of the postal clerk, he now knows that he wasn't lacking some special conversational 'gift'. All he needed was a bit of direction and confidence in how simple it is to generate and implant 'things to say' in his mind. He left the session eager to create new habit patterns of conversational success and start putting these into practice.

REDUCE IDEAS INTO DEFINITE THINGS TO SAY

When you read an article, or see a documentary or movie and so forth, boil your overall impressions down into one or two definite things to say. Make it a habit to read the movie blurbs when they're advertised or even the information provided when they're on TV to see how cleverly reviewers condense their impressions down into one or two sentences. In Step 5 (see chapter 9), you'll discover that specific comments tossed in here and there help carry the conversation forward.

Starting a conversation file

As mentioned earlier, write down your memories, impressions and snippets of information, which of course include your personal anecdotes, and file them under specific headings for easy access.

The following headings cover most topics of conversation:

- Animals
- Art
- Books
- Children
- Entertainment
- Environment

- Fashions
- Hobbies
- Holidays
- Humour
- Music
- News
- People
- Sport
- Technology

Regularly review, discard items and add others to this file.

IN A NUTSHELL

- Cultivate a thirst for knowledge.

- Get enthusiastic about the world around you and continually look for connections.

- If you're wondering 'why?', don't leave it – find out why using the internet, or by another means.

- Reduce your ideas and impressions into definite things to say.

- File ideas and snippets under specific headings for easy access.

CHAPTER 6

Step 2:
Define your purpose

Unlike a set piece of written work, where everything can be thought out beforehand and then written to this plan, we have no idea where spontaneous conversation is going to take us. Therefore, our purpose can only be of a general nature. On social occasions or impromptu situations where we have little time for forethought, our general purpose of being a pleasant, agreeable person should always be our aim. You'll find it much more pleasurable – and profitable – to have people experience you as an agreeable person, rather than someone who rubs people up the wrong way and is hard to get along with.

On other occasions, it pays to have a clearly defined purpose clearly in your mind. So jot this down in a single, definite sentence beforehand.

For example, consider the following situations and the possible purpose for the chat:

- With a slight acquaintance, the purpose could be, 'To be pleasant and agreeable and get to know this person better'.

- With an intimate friend, the purpose could be, 'To keep them informed of your activities'.

- With an unreasonable colleague at work, the purpose could be, 'To make your working relationship as pleasant as possible'.

- In a job interview, the purpose could be, 'To come across as a confident and enthusiastic person who has done some research on what the company is about'.

Having a clear idea of where you want the conversation to go will help you avoid any rough water and safely steer it there.

IN A NUTSHELL

- Approach any conversation that is important to you with a clearly formulated purpose in your mind.

- Always strive to be a pleasant, agreeable person.

CHAPTER 7

Step 3:
Remember names

Someone once said that the sweetest sound we can hear is the mention of our name. Yet, we've all been in the situation where someone has introduced us to a group of people and the whole thing has seemed like a blur. How embarrassing when an individual of that same group later remembers your name and you can't remember theirs! Here's how to avoid this embarrassing predicament.

CATCH THE NAME CLEARLY

If the name is tossed at you carelessly, don't hesitate to say, 'I'm sorry, I didn't catch your name.' No-one will mind you showing an interest in their name. Repeat it slowly and distinctly so it will register.

If necessary, sidle up to a friend and ask if they remember a particular person's name. This ploy will enable you to later approach the person and drop their name into the conversation with confidence.

WORK ON DIFFICULT NAMES

In today's multicultural society, we are apt to meet people from a great variety of backgrounds. Hearing a name that's difficult for you spelt out, as well as pronounced, will allow you to better get hold of it. Play it back to them. The person to whom you've been introduced will appreciate your concern in getting their name right. This exercise also acts as a wonderful icebreaker.

USE THE PERSON'S NAME

During the course of the conversation use the person's name as often as you reasonably can. Instead of saying, 'Did you arrive today or last night?' say, 'Did you arrive today or last night, Bill?' This not only puts the other person at ease, but also helps set their name firmly in your mind. (Just don't overdo it!)

ASSOCIATE THE NAME WITH SOMETHING FAMILIAR

If you're finding a new name hard to remember, make a mental association with something familiar that borders on the absurd. The more ridiculous, the easier the name becomes to remember.

For example, with my name, Laurie Smale, you could picture a large truck hauling a gigantic snail: 'Lorry snail'. That's an image not easy to forget. To this day, I clearly remember Eddie Van Eeden, who I briefly met some 50 years ago, simply because of the ridiculous picture I conjured up at the time. I can see smiling Eddie now, sitting in the back of an open white 'van', wearing a huge pair of Mickey Mouse 'ears', before the whole thing disappears into a lion's 'den' – with their roars in the background to add to the atmospherics! Eddie Van Ee (ear) den. Even after all these years, this ridiculous mental-jogging scenario has been hard to shake.

REAP THE BENEFITS

With a little effort, you'll find all this will become second nature for you'll be forming new habits. Chances are, if you bump into this new acquaintance a few days later, you'll be able to effortlessly say, 'Hello Eddie, nice to see you again! I'm Laurie Smale. We met at the club the other night.'

Eddie will not only be thrilled you remembered his name, but also appreciate the thoughtful way you helped him to remember yours. The ability to remember a person's name with confidence is an important step along the path to conversational success. It's not a gift – it's a skill that you can easily develop.

Remember my name and
you add to my feeling of importance.

Dale Carnegie

IN A NUTSHELL

- If you don't catch a name clearly, ask the person to repeat it so it can register.

- Hearing a name you find difficult spelt out as well as pronounced will allow you to firmly get hold of it.

- During the course of the conversation, use the person's name often.

- Associate the name with something familiar. The more ridiculous this association, the easier it is to remember.

- Make it easy for the other person to remember your name.

CHAPTER 8

Step 4:
Start a conversation

From the outset, it's crucial you understand that it's perfectly normal to feel a little awkward when we first meet people we don't know. Everyone feels this way.

But if you really want to talk to a particular person, nothing is going to happen until you pluck up the courage, walk over and say something! This chapter provides some tried-and-proven tips to help you break the ice and get things moving.

BREAK THE ICE YOURSELF

One good way to help people relax in a group of like-minded people is to reach out and introduce yourself: 'Hi, I don't think we've met before. I'm Mary Johnson.' Another icebreaker I often use is, 'And where do you fit into the picture? Are you a friend of Samuel's?' Comment on what you have in common, no matter how flimsy the link may be: 'Looks like we're the only ones who didn't get the message about formal dress!' The secret is not to try to be too clever with the first thing you say. Small talk is the key. People feel relieved when someone strikes up a conversation with something light like the weather or the number of people in attendance, or a particular setting. Small talk is non-threatening and helps people settle in and contribute to the conversation.

COMMENT ON THE OBVIOUS

If it's bucketing down outside don't ignore it. Make an observation like, 'Great day to be out!' You'll find a quip like this will immediately break the tension and everyone will have some light-hearted comment to make. If you notice something of interest as you enter, comment on it. 'I was wondering about that magnificent cat asleep on the porch. Is it Burmese or Siamese?' Ten to one this will stimulate a comment from someone and the conversation will be up and running.

BE PREPARED

One of the best ways to ensure you're armed with an opening wedge or two is to find out as much as you can beforehand about the person or persons you're about to meet. 'I believe your daughter is a netball champion', or 'They tell me you're an avid fisherman' will probably tap into a passion the other person is eager to expand upon.

Sometimes the opportunity to gain 'inside' information is limited. I remember my wife and I were once invited to a couple's house for dinner. About all I knew of them was that their surname was Sterling. This sparked off an idea. After the introductions and those first few awkward moments, we settled in with some small talk. During this light conversation, I made the comment, 'Your surname intrigues me. It doesn't happen to stem from a family of money makers or bankers by any chance?' Well, everyone laughed and we spent the next half-hour or so absorbed in the probable origin of everyone's name.

PUT PEOPLE AT EASE

One sure way to wet blanket a conversation before it even begins is to subject the other person to personal questions.

By all means, lend an ear when necessary, but don't pry. Uninvited personal questions antagonise. Keep it light and friendly by asking the other person their opinion on impersonal topics. Most of us feel comfortable in expressing some point of view when talking to strangers if asked our opinion on something we feel at ease with and that is familiar to us.

GO EASY ON YOUR TROUBLES AND WOES

We all experience emotional ups and downs. We might have recently achieved a lifelong dream, or be going through a rough patch in our lives. There will be a time when it's appropriate to draw on this information to keep conversation going – but that time is not the moment we meet somebody.

I once turned to a fellow passenger on a plane and said, 'Where are you headed?'

'Sydney,' he replied. Then the floodgates opened. In the space of three minutes I discovered that his wife had left him, his car had conked out on the freeway, and he was probably headed for the sack when he arrived in Sydney. He then fell silent. The conversation had come to an abrupt end.

Luckily, I had the techniques of 'keeping the conversation going' at my disposal (you'll learn more about this in step 5, chapter 9) and tactfully pulled the conversation out of the emotional doldrums. The fascinating thing was this guy had once attempted to climb Mt Everest! You can imagine how interesting the conversation became once I discovered that! But when we did say our goodbyes as we exited the plane, I made a point of saying to him, 'I hope things all work out for you in a positive way.'

My point is this: friendly agreeable chitchat at the start of a conversation will encourage people to stick around and enjoy your company. The conversation may indeed become more deep and meaningful, but launch into a barrage of your troubles and woes straightaway and they'll likely run a mile.

REFLECT THE FEELINGS OF THE MOMENT

Now that you know it's not good practice to blurt out your entire life story the moment you meet someone, and that commonsense and sensitivity should be your guiding light, you may well be asking, 'How do I maintain my distance and prevent myself from getting too close to a person during the rest of the conversation?'

You don't. Conversation should be a dynamic living thing, able to reflect the feelings of the moment. In fact, I try to make it easy for people to share a little of themselves with me. Here's how I go about it.

After some non-threatening small talk, I'll personalise my observations with something of relevance that happened to me. For example, we could be commenting on a formidably steep hill at the front of the premises. I could muse on how it reminds me of just how fearless we were as kids, and how we used to hurtle down a similar hill in a billycart, totally unafraid of the consequences. This kind of casual observation brings the discussion down to a personal level and helps you connect with the human side of life that we all have in common. It also acts as a stimulus, giving the other person permission to share something similar with you that they have experienced. Before you know it, the dynamics of conversation have taken over. You're soon feeding off each other's experiences, relating to one another, and the concept of maintaining your distance is no longer a concern.

IN A NUTSHELL

- Don't try to be too clever with your initial comment. Small talk is the key.

- If something of interest catches your eye as you enter, comment on it.

- Find out as much as you can beforehand about the person or persons you're about to meet.

- Don't pry. Keep the conversation light and friendly at first by asking the other person their opinion on impersonal topics.

- Encourage others to enjoy your company. Go easy on your troubles and woes.

- Relate to one another by feeding off each other's experiences.

CHAPTER 9

Step 5:
Keep the conversation going

You don't have to be a walking encyclopaedia or a non-stop talker to keep a conversation from flagging; after all, we can't know everything. In fact, you can use these 'gaps of knowledge' to keep the conversation going. Here we introduce another vital element to conversation effectiveness: showing genuine interest in the other person and considering the manner in which you listen to them.

> *No man would listen to you talk*
> *if he didn't know it was his turn next.*
>
> Edgar Watson Howe

USE ACTIVE LISTENING

Unlike the completely passive listener – with whom it's an endless struggle to elicit any sort of reaction – the active listener is alive, alert and contributes to the conversation. Their eyes don't impatiently glance away. They reflect a sincere interest in what you have to say and an eagerness to expand their knowledge and learn from your experiences. The spotlight is fairly and squarely on you and your interests and they encourage you to talk about yourself.

When the active listener speaks, it's to carry the conversation forward by way of an occasional observation, exclamation or question. For example:

- 'I remember reading something about that in the paper yesterday.'
- 'I'll bet that was tough.'
- 'You are kidding!'
- 'Isn't that like saying …'
- 'How on earth did you get back?'

Active listening is also about making connections – for example, when something dawns on you, you may say something like, 'You mean they went without her?'

The sparkling conversationalist, therefore, actively listens to what the other person is saying and kicks discussion along with an occasional comment or realisation.

SHARE SILENCE

At times, however, not much needs be said at all – yet the communication continues. Admiring a scene of great beauty such as a magnificent sunset or consoling someone in time of need are examples of non-verbal conversation. Here we become sharers of silence while the message remains crystal clear.

Silence can be golden …

… On other occasions, silence can be deafening.

One guy told me how he felt he was a conversational failure simply because the chap he was travelling with sat slumped in the airport lounge chair too dog-tired to speak. They'd just spent 12 hours straight on a plane and his usually talkative companion was all out of energy. The last thing on his mind was to get involved in a lively conversation!

Yet our friend took this as a personal rejection, reinforcing his long-held notion that he was a lousy conversationalist. 'If only I'd had something interesting to say,' he later told me. I pointed out that effective conversation does not mean we've got to keep on talking for talk's sake. We've also got to be aware of how the other person feels and know when to shut up. At times, silence can indeed be golden.

ALLOW CHAIN REACTIONS

Isn't it interesting how a piece of music, a certain smell, or an idea can get us thinking about something that has laid dormant within us for years? The successful conversationalist is well aware of this undeniable fact. They know that in a relaxed setting where conversation is left to free-range over the landscape of our minds, one subject will invariably suggest another.

Recently my wife and I spent a memorable evening with some friends for dinner. In the space of three hours our conversation covered everything from the smoked trout in the hors d'oeuvres to *just* what *is* under a Scotsman's kilt! Similar to a chain reaction, each mental image set us off on some other tangent, introducing a new topic for us to talk about.

Make connections

Closely akin to these 'chain reactions' are the connections we make with things we are not so familiar with. As with the bits of a puzzle, each piece of new information builds on what we already know and furthers our understanding of the overall picture.

For example, on a three-hour journey I once found myself companion to a scientist who specialised in the development and running of sewerage farms. What to talk about? I knew next to nothing about his vocation. By employing the principles of active listening, however, that potentially boring journey turned out to be absolutely fascinating. He was eager to share his passion with someone who displayed such genuine interest, and we ended up covering everything from the design of a sewerage farm to the bugs that reconstitute human waste into clean water. I'm not exaggerating when I say he had me enthralled. But it was a two-way street for there's a lot of truth in the saying, 'Talk to someone about themselves and they'll listen for hours'.

My questions mirrored his enthusiasm, and one of my questions was, 'Can you market all the sludge that's left over as fertiliser?'

He shook his head. 'Unfortunately, we can't do anything with it. Too many heavy metals such as cadmium, lead, and zinc.

At this stage, we have no way of extracting them and the non-usable sludge just stays heaped up in the paddocks.'

Years later, I was talking to an electrician in Sydney who had just won a contract to install the latest computerised machinery from Germany specifically designed to extract heavy metals from sewerage sludge. This new information reawakened the lengthy conversation I'd had with my scientific travelling companion all those years ago. This incredible machinery could render those hitherto useless heaps of poisoned sludge into non-toxic potting mix of the highest quality – and make a profit with the retrieved metals! As we talked, I was able to relate to this electrician's world with brief reflective references that had been filed away in my subconscious from my much earlier conversation on sewerage management.

It really is exciting when we make these little connections and another piece of a given puzzle falls into place. This expansion of previous information gives us audible 'realisations' to toss into the conversation and help it to move along.

Talk to them about frogs

Let's look at one more example of how to keep a conversation going even if you know little about the topic.

I distinctly recall a conversation I once had with a distinguished-looking gentleman on a social occasion. After plucking up the courage to walk over and say hello, I casually asked him what he did with his time.

'I'm with the CSIRO, and at the moment I'm working on a project categorising frogs.' Well, at other times in my life this would have stumped me. I would have just stood there, completely ill at ease with nothing to say. Not anymore.

Now that I have myself right, my mind is free to focus 100 per cent on the other person and what they are saying. I'm free to trust my mind to retrieve some relevant piece of information from the billions of bits and pieces that are floating around in there just waiting to be activated. Without even thinking, I found myself saying, 'Aren't frogs a bit like environmental barometers? Similar to the canaries in the olden-day coalmines?'

Well, I struck oil for away he went! I'd tapped into something this man cared deeply about. All I had to do now was show a genuine interest in what he was saying with an occasional comment to keep things ticking along. I tossed questions and comments into the conversation at the appropriate time as they miraculously came to the forefront of my mind. Such as the following:

- 'What about snakes?'
- 'I was watching a documentary about some rare yellowish frog that's disappearing from around the Daintree River. Do you know about that?'
- 'I remember catching tadpoles as a kid where thousands of them were left to die as their shallow ponds dried up, does that affect numbers?'
- 'Kids today would rather sit by their computers – maybe we can use computers to keep them in touch with nature?'

And on it went for a good 20 minutes!

Remember – he did most of the talking and I did most of the listening. All I did was subtly egg him on.

So if a person is interested in frogs, talk to them about frogs!

My problem then became not what to say, but how to tactfully end this interesting conversation when I had to. You'll learn how to effectively close a conversation in Step 8 (in chapter 12).

KEEP CONVERSATION IN PLACID WATERS

If someone threatens to take over the conversation and steer it into unpleasant or embarrassing waters, wait until they have finished speaking and then tactfully use a cut-in remark to change the subject.

For example, 'Perhaps it's not a good idea that we talk about this without all the information before us. We could be barking up the wrong tree!' or 'Does anyone know what's happening with the function next week?' Usually someone will be alert enough to pick up on this 'safer' topic and run with it.

Although a mild reproof, note that the first example used the phrase, 'It's not a good idea that *we* talk about this', instead of '*you* talk about this'. Though this tactless person should have known better, the pronoun 'we' doesn't single anybody out and prevents feelings being hurt. Whether justified or not, using 'we' puts everyone in the same boat. Note also that the light-hearted nature of the cut-in remark seeks to maintain a friendly, agreeable atmosphere.

Avoid generalisations

Don't make sweeping generalisations if you are not familiar with every single person in the group – for example, 'All accountants are boring.' An accountant might be present or a member of the group might be married to one!

Throw out a lifeline

If someone inadvertently says the wrong thing or innocently does something embarrassing, throw them a lifeline.

During an animated passage of conversation, I once spilt a glass of red wine over our host's expensive white linen table-cloth. Mortified, I expressed my profound apologies. The conversation we were previously enjoying was now completely forgotten.

Once the commotion had died down and the hostess had poured a heap of salt on this glaring red stain, a fellow dinner companion came to my rescue. He told the story of when he was courting his wife to be (who happened to be the hostess), and how he had the embarrassing habit of regularly knocking his glass of wine over whenever invited to her parents' place for dinner.

In the end, they did away with a tablecloth altogether and used plastic placemats instead. He said it didn't cure his clumsiness but it was easier to mop up the inevitable mess!

You can imagine how the thoughtfulness of that story took the focus off me and eased a lot of my embarrassment. Everyone enjoyed it, the conversation again gathered momentum and the incident was put to one side.

SENSE THE MOOD OF THE MOMENT

A colleague and I were once engaged in light and friendly conversation with a group of storytellers when an agitated woman burst in on the scene and exclaimed, 'Oh, it was awful! No-one paid attention, nothing was organised, and I was left to fend for myself!'

We just stood there wondering who the hell she was and what it was all about. The mood was shattered and the friendly atmosphere we had been enjoying a moment earlier instantly became morbid and serious. Her insensitivity had effectively killed our conversation stone dead.

It is vital, therefore, when joining a group engaged in conversation you first tune in to the mood of the moment instead of heedlessly barging in with what you have to say and get everyone off side. Always be ready to put your passion aside and approach things from a lighter angle in a more feeling way.

AVOID INSIGNIFICANT DETAILS

A sure-fire way to switch people off is to get bogged down in insignificant details.

You've no doubt suffered this sort of thing: 'I remember last Tuesday … No, I tell a lie, it was Thursday. On second thoughts, it could have been Wednesday … Anyway, Sarah pulls up in this bright red convertible … Well, when I say red, it was probably more pink than red, sort of like a sunset. Anyway she walks in through the main door … No, again I tell a lie! It was the side door … And she puts this box down on the bench, or was it the table?'

And on it drones, the speaker's listeners drifting aimlessly in a sea of unimportant details. They really don't care if it was Tuesday or Wednesday, or whether the car was red or pink, or whether Sarah entered through the front or side door, or whether it was the table or the bench. They just want to know what happened! To be interesting, therefore, don't be a detail bore. Your listeners will fill in the rest of the picture themselves.

Let's look at this example again: 'I remember last Tuesday, Sarah pulls up in a bright red convertible, walks in through the main door, and dumps a box of stuff on the table!' If you want to maintain interest, go easy on the trivial details. Stick to the essential facts and get people involved in the action.

KEEP EVERYONE IN THE CONVERSATION

Of course, focusing on the outward personalities and good talkers of the group so they may shine works well. But it's equally important to create an opportunity for those less forward individuals to share their opinion with an unobtrusive cut-in remark. 'We've all been rattling out heads off about the places we've been in Australia … Joan, you've just spent some time bush walking in Tasmania. How did you find it?'

We all have a feeling of importance when invited to share an experience we've recently enjoyed or our thoughts on the subject under discussion.

Put them in the picture

Likewise, when a newcomer joins the group, make them feel at home. Don't bamboozle them with in-house jargon, seldom-used terms or in-jokes, and don't continue the conversation and ignore them. Have them feel welcome and put them in the picture. 'This in Annette Gibson, she manages the local plant nursery. Annette, we're in the middle of a trekking expedition in the Himalayas!'

This serves two purposes: the comment 'She manages the local plant nursery' gives members of the group an opening wedge to later start a conversation with Annette, and she feels welcome and part of the conversation.

TAKE THE HINT

Politeness is an inexpensive way of making friends but not every person we meet is going to be pleasant and agreeable. Occasionally, for whatever reason, a particular individual doesn't want to play the conversation game. They might be like that by nature or they might have recently experienced something momentous in their lives. Whatever the reason, don't take their behaviour personally – and, in particular, don't let it reinforce the ill-founded notion that you're a conversational dud.

They might grunt in reply to your friendly overtures or simply ignore you. They might pretend not to see your friendly smile and look straight through you. Their response has little to do with you as a person, and even less does it prove you are a conversational failure. You've played your part in being a pleasant, agreeable person. That's all you can do. Take the hint and leave them to their solitude.

IN A NUTSHELL

- Keep the spotlight squarely on others and radiate genuine interest.

- Actively listen to what the other person is saying.

- Play on the 'chain reaction effect', where one related idea sets off another.

- As a penny drops and you make connections, verbalise your realisations out loud. This spurs on the other person to elaborate further.

- If the conversation enters unpleasant or embarrassing waters, take the plunge and tactfully change the subject with a cut-in remark.

- Avoid sweeping generalisations.

- If someone inadvertently says the wrong thing or does something embarrassing, throw them a lifeline.

- When joining a group engaged in conversation, tune into the mood of the moment before you speak.

- Stick to the bare facts and action of a story. Don't be a detail bore.

- Create opportunities for less forward people to express themselves.

- Acknowledge newcomers and put them in the picture.

- If an individual doesn't want to play the conversation game, don't take it personally. Take the hint and leave them to their solitude.

CHAPTER 10

Step 6:
Handle an interview

Assuming that you're appropriately dressed for the interview and have armed yourself with a professionally prepared CV, here are some other tips to ensure you're among the likely contenders as you near the winning post.

CARRY YOURSELF WITH CONFIDENCE

Be aware that the interviewer likely feels a little awkward and nervous too, even though they mightn't show it. Accept the fact that it's normal for everyone to feel a bit uncomfortable in an interview setting. And be prepared to engage in a bit of small talk to break the ice.

Remember that interviews cost time and money, and the person behind the desk is not out to get you or trip you up in any way. Hopefully, you are just the person they're looking for!

So carry yourself with the quiet confidence of someone who believes they're the person for the job.

RESEARCH THE COMPANY BEFOREHAND

Before you even think of leaving for the interview, get online and find out as much as you can about the company. That way, in answer to the question, 'What do you know about our company?' you'll be able to impress the interviewer with some intelligent comment relating to the organisation – commenting, perhaps, on their recent expansion into South-East Asia, their restructuring program, or the new plant they've just opened in Melbourne.

Fundamental preparation such as this will put you well in front of other contenders for the job.

STUDY THE JOB REQUIREMENTS

Carefully consider the job requirements in the ad to determine your strengths and weaknesses with regard to this particular position. These are the main things the interviewer will be focusing on. If asked, use specific examples from your experiences to illustrate you understand the essence of each requirement. For those areas you're not as good at, let them know you learn fast and don't see it as a problem. Give them an example of where you've experienced the requirement under discussion somewhere else – for example, an illustration of the initiative you had to show when working in the kitchen at McDonald's would be ideal.

A young lady I know once applied for a job as a firefighter with Victoria's Metropolitan Fire Brigade. One of the job requirements was being able to 'think clearly in time of crisis'. When asked by the interviewer to illustrate what this meant to her, she replied with a story. When she was a teenager, Ashley was often given the daunting responsibility of milking the 200 cows on her parents' dairy farm in time of need or emergency.

This particular day, her parents had had to make the long trip to Melbourne, and so the milking was up to Ashley. Everything was going fine, with cows hooked up to the milking machines and contentedly chewing their cuds. All of a sudden, the boards of one of the elevated platforms on which the cows were standing gave way and sent one of the prized Jersey's back legs crashing through a gaping hole. With no time to reflect on the gravity of the situation, 15-year-old Ashley went into action.

Although badly cut and scratched, Strawberry's legs had landed on a concrete wall directly beneath the shattered platform. Ashley quickly released the holding bar from across the frightened cow's neck, released the cups from her udder, and with a great deal of pushing and shoving somehow coaxed Strawberry to lift her legs out of this lethal trap.

When her parents arrived home, they were astonished to learn that not only had Ashley's quick thinking rescued one of their prize milkers, she'd also calmly gone on to finish milking the entire herd!

The interviewer must have been impressed with this response, for Ashley was duly accepted into the rigorous training course and went on to become a professional firefighter.

PRACTISE PREPARED SPONTANEITY

A key factor in whether you get the job or not is your proficiency in handling people. So revisit that personal well of wisdom and self-esteem we established in part 1. Search out your real-life experiences that show you as a team player, your reliability, how you get along with others, and your leadership qualities. Prepare something specific to say on each of these 'people' qualities. You may not need them, but then again you may. I call this 'prepared spontaneity'.

You may illustrate the qualities of persistence and reliability with an example of how you put yourself through university with a part-time job. Or you could demonstrate how you are slow to anger by replaying a recent incident where you had every reason to blow your top but didn't.

ANTICIPATE UNUSUAL QUESTIONS

Also be ready for unusual questions. In answer to the question, 'What do you see as your strengths?', you might reply, 'I feel I get along well with people and would make a good team member.' You would, of course, be able to expand on this with a specific example that illustrates the point if asked to do so.

Conversely, if you were thrown the question, 'And what do you see as an area you need to work on?' you could well be in trouble. Here's how to get around it.

No-one is perfect, so you've got to own up to something! But make sure the human frailty you select is harmless and in no way jeopardises your chances of getting the job. When the interviewer leaned back in his chair and threw me the question,

'What do you see as your main weakness?', for example, I told him that my enthusiasm sometimes gets the better of me and I tend to forget that others have valuable ideas to contribute as well as me. But I also highlighted there's always a little man on my shoulder saying, 'Hold back a minute and listen to what they've got to say!' This way I turned a negative into a positive by demonstrating that I'm continually working on being a good listener! In other words, my 'problem' of being over-enthusiastic is under control and no longer a concern.

Not long back one of my daughters went for a job interview. When asked the question, 'And what do you see as one of your weaknesses?' she said, 'Well, I'm a bit worried about a couple of aspects of the job; like do I have to know how to fill in all the forms straightaway?'

'Oh, don't worry about that,' the interviewer said. 'You'll get lots of training in all that stuff.'

Satisfied with her response, the interviewer moved on. And yes, she did get the job.

She told me later that she'd prepared her response based on the likelihood of this question being asked before she went for the interview. Make sure you do the same.

REHEARSE THE INTERVIEW 'LIVE'

I would never speak in front of an audience or conduct a workshop or one-on-one coaching session without first running through the whole thing in my mind.

Preparing for an interview is exactly the same. Here's how to make the unexpected expected: for five to ten minutes a day, for a few days before the interview, sit down in a quiet corner and actually 'see' the interviewers in front of you and how they're reacting to what you're saying in response to their questions about specific job requirements. Don't be concerned with the exact words you use, unless they're key phrases or terminology you'd use for effect; just mull over your main ideas for each requirement and let the words intuitively flow as they would in normal conversation. Some of this preparation is out loud; most of it will be in your head.

Especially concentrate on all possible questions the interviewers could throw at you, and select key ideas and examples with which to answer these inquiries. Write them down on bits of paper and then jumble them up and pick one of these questions out at random. Confidently answer the question in a conversational way with your prepared example as if the interviewer is sitting there with you. Don't try to remember these responses word for word, because they have to come across as spontaneous and natural. This way, each time you answer these questions the words will be ever so slightly different. Only now are you ready to attend the interview and interact with the interviewer with confidence! If a particular meeting or interview is important to you, you should rehearse it 'live' beforehand every time.

These few minutes of rehearsal time each day for a week or so will create an internal comfort zone within yourself so you're in control of the situation and ready for anything the interviewers might throw at you.

IN A NUTSHELL

- Break the ice in an interview with small talk.

- Carry yourself with the quiet confidence of someone who believes in themself.

- Learn as much as you can about the organisation before the interview.

- Arm yourself with specific incidents and examples of your positive 'people' qualities.

- Prepare a response to the questions 'What do you see as your strengths?' and 'What is an area you need to work on?'

- Create an internal comfort zone within yourself by rehearsing the interview 'live'.

CHAPTER 11

Step 7:
Make the most of
networking opportunities

We've all seen the networking 'junkies', flitting around from person to person singing their own praises and scattering their business cards like bits of confetti. The more people they get to, the better. If only they knew. Most of their precious business cards will end up in the wastebasket.

SOW THE SEEDS OF A RELATIONSHIP

True networking is all about staying with someone long enough to get to know them a little and establish the seeds of a relationship, not 'working' the whole room. International speaker Glenna Salsbury, former President of the National Speakers Association of America, claimed she did no traditional marketing as such, yet she was in constant demand as a speaker. She said, 'I get there early, stay late, and get to know people.' What priceless advice! After all – people buy people first, and then your products or services. So don't be in a rush to get away. Stick around. Get to know people and sow the seeds of a few relationships.

FOCUS ON PEOPLE OF INFLUENCE

While it's true we never know who we might meet at a gathering, if your specific purpose is to generate business or become known or promote some cause, why not introduce yourself to people of influence? We've already discovered that under the surface notable people are very much like everyone else. And it is nice to be able to phone a prospective client the following day and say, 'I was talking to your President, John Thompson, last night and he suggested I give you a call.' (Naturally, you would have asked John's permission to mention his name.)

In his bestselling book *Ready, Aim, Sell!*, Michael Harrison, professional speaker and life member of the Million Dollar Round Table (a global association of financial professionals), recalls one of his first calls in insurance was to a man he'd heard was very wealthy.

'He was in his 60s, successful and probably uninsurable. He was also extremely influential. We chatted about all sorts of things, especially the good my products could do for people. He ended up introducing me to dozens of people. Because of his personal prestige and wealth, they were delighted to take his recommendation to see me.'

ESTABLISH A SENSE OF TRUST

If you sense a too-good-to-miss opportunity with the person you're talking to, resist the temptation to launch into a business proposition right there and then. You won't get far unless you first tread some common ground together and establish a platform of trust. So keep the conversation focused on the other person and their interests, with an occasional insight into what it is you do and how it might help them.

Then again, you might have them saying right up-front, 'You're just the person who can help me!' In this case, listen carefully to their reasons as to why this is so, and then question them further on their specific situation before you proffer any solutions!

You'll thus be able to tailor what you say to suit their needs and so whet their appetite to want to know more.

ELIMINATE COLD CALL REJECTIONS

At the end of a networking conversation, say something like, 'It'd be nice to catch up for a chat over coffee sometime and explore a few ideas.' The suggestion of a 'chat over coffee' is less pushy and friendlier than trying to arrange a meeting. It also shows that you respect the fact that they are busy and you don't intend to waste their time. Remember at this stage your objective should simply be to create rapport and establish a relationship. As you part company, say you'll give them a call next week sometime to organise a date.

Be sure to write the essence of the conversation in point form on the back of their card or in your electronic device at your earliest opportunity. You'll find this information will help you remember who the person is, their interests, and what it is they do. Now you'll have something in common to talk about when you follow them up.

But before phoning them, first send a friendly email or text stating what a pleasure it was to meet them, adding that you'll be calling in a day or so to arrange a date for that 'chat over coffee'. When you talk to them again you'll be talking to a friend, helping to eliminate the fear of a cold call rejection.

SEEK OUT LIKE-MINDED PEOPLE

Here's a further way to reduce the networking odds in your favour. I was once talking to a chap who had recently started a home-based business rewiring swimming pool motors. I said, 'That's interesting. Who's your target market? People who own a pool, or actual pool shops?'

He hesitated, 'Both. It's a relatively small niche – though things are a bit tough at the moment because it's seasonal.'

I said, 'Why don't you talk to electricians, pool manufacturers, and other people in the business?'

He showed little enthusiasm for this suggestion. 'I've tried that and they all seem happy with their suppliers. Anyway it's virtually impossible to break into their circle.' In effect, he was sitting at home waiting for the phone to ring.

I then suggested he try frequenting meetings and exhibitions of like-minded people related to his business, such as Master Electricians Australia. Here he wouldn't be focusing only on swimming pool motors but all kinds of electric motors.

His eyes lit up. He hadn't thought of this obvious line of action. Here was a whole room full of people with a potential need of his services! He'd feel at home in this environment because he'd have something in common with anyone he spoke to. He caught hold of the notion of complementing their existing service by offering himself as a 24-hour emergency supplier.

I explained that the trick is to go along as a guest at first. Acknowledge old friends, sure, but mostly focus on people he'd never met before and get to know them.

I then got him thinking about creating his own internet presence to make his services known. He could then create links of mutual benefit with other related entities to generate even more interest in what he was doing. Now he was all fired up because he was in control and doing something with real people. Now he was heading somewhere.

HUMANISE YOUR BUSINESS CARD

Let's stop here for a moment and return to the heart of the matter. Why should anyone follow you up after a meeting to enquire further about your services? The simple answer is because they liked you and enjoyed your company. They liked the way you related to them and their world. They liked the way you engendered trust and made them feel important. And, of course, they liked the way you could help them in some way.

Now your business card has a human face and means something to them. They'd feel guilty tossing you in the wastebasket like a piece of rubbish. So they file you away with the important cards they frequently use. And isn't this what you do with the cards of friendly people who leave a lasting impression on you? Isn't this how you expand your own personal network of friends and business associates?

HANDLE 'CLIQUEY' GROUPS

I'm often asked, 'But what if the group is "cliquey" and they all seem to know one another? This can be really intimidating!'

Sure it can. And this is exactly how I felt when I first became a member of the National Speakers Association of Australia many years ago. A bit like Max Hitchins as a country lad (refer to chapter 1), I'd initially stand on the outskirts of the crowd feeling very uncomfortable, afraid that if I joined some group I might be ignored. So I'd seek out other 'fringe dwellers' who seemed to be in need of company.

Invariably our mutual newness to the situation gave us something in common to talk about. From there, I cultivated friendships and respect. In next to no time my perceived feelings of being left out evaporated and I was able to move comfortably within the group. This connects with what I've touched on through this book: I generate a great deal of business by approaching the 'fringe dwellers' at a gathering. I strongly suggest you do the same.

Margaret Seedsman, a colleague of mine, takes a slightly different tack. She says that when she is among a group of people who are a bit 'cliquey', she *deliberately* stands alone and waits for people to come to her! (She prefers to stand near the coffee machine.) Margaret says it never fails. 'Someone always comes over to say hello.'

So within any given group of people, no matter what your first impressions may be, you'll always find someone in there eager to talk to you. The secret is to hang back a little and gently feel your way into the group.

ASK FOR REFERRALS

One last thing: once people are sold on what you do and appreciate you as a trustworthy person, they usually don't mind referring you to other people in your target market. So as Michael Harrison suggests earlier in this chapter, always ask if they know anyone else who could benefit from your products and services. This personal link with someone who respects you will enable you to approach their referrals with confidence.

Now, with a friendly smile and the techniques outlined in this book, you'll be able to make the most of all your networking opportunities.

IN A NUTSHELL

- If your purpose is to generate business or become known, approach people of influence to have a chat with.

- Be sure to tread some common ground together and establish a sense of trust before you outline any business proposal.

- The suggestion of a 'chat over coffee' is less pushy and friendlier than trying to set up a business meeting.

- Write the essence of the conversation in point form on the back of their business card or on your device so you'll have something to talk about when you follow them up. Now you'll be talking to a friend, helping to eliminate the fear of a cold call rejection.

- Frequent meetings and associations of like-minded people related to your business. Here you'll have a gathering of potential customers!

- If alone, seek out other 'fringe dwellers' who seem to be in need of company. Your mutual uneasiness will help you relate to one another and give you something to talk about.

- Once you've delivered your service and earned the other person's trust and respect, ask for referrals.

CHAPTER 12

Step 8:
Close a conversation

Being a pleasant, agreeable person, you've patiently listened to a lengthy but interesting description of a recent gall bladder operation and it's time to move on. How do you extricate yourself without hurting this person?

Easy – politely say you need a drink, or want to grab a sandwich before they all go, or say hello to someone across the room, or catch a train (and so on). And you don't have to make these things up. If there's an ounce of truth in what you're saying, it will ring true. It really is that simple. And the more you practise, the easier it gets. As you move away, say something like, 'It's been nice talking to you … I hope you're better soon.' With this little strategy up your sleeve, you'll be able to give everyone you have a chat with the time of day. Your mind will be free to genuinely become part of what the other person is saying, instead of concentrating on *How am I going to get out of this?!* You'll not only be friendly to be with, but also brighten up their day. And again, you never know what pleasant surprises may stem from a little patience, tolerance and understanding.

CLOSING AN EMOTIONAL CONVERSATION

In times of emotion, a slight touch on the other person's shoulder or arm can help release you from a conversation without hurting their feelings.

Some time back I had just finished giving a talk on 'The Art of Conversation', when some members of my audience invited me to join them for coffee. I readily accepted their kind offer and told them I'd be with them shortly.

Their spokesman said, 'We'll order it for you and see you downstairs.'

As I was packing my bag, another chap came up and expressed how much he had enjoyed my talk and what it meant to him. He became quite intense as he explained his transition from war-torn Bosnia to his new life here in Australia. The more I listened, the more I became involved in the conversation.

Although he had my complete attention, in the back of my mind I was aware that I'd promised to join the folks downstairs for coffee.

I listened carefully for another two minutes or so, and then, during a pause, I reached out and touched this emotional man on the shoulder. Looking him square in the eyes I said, 'Tom, I'd love to finish this conversation with you sometime, but I've got some people waiting for me downstairs for coffee.'

He then defended me! 'No, that's fine. It's been a pleasure talking to you. Please enjoy your coffee.' And we parted the warmest of friends.

DON'T OVERSTAY YOUR WELCOME

If at someone's place for dinner and you sense that it's time to go, it's up to you to make the first move in taking your leave – not the host. Respect the fact that everyone has their own agenda to consider. Say something like, 'Time's getting on' or 'We must be going', and then get up.

They'll of course play the courtesy game of 'Oh, must you? Why don't you have another cup of coffee?' But don't fall for it! Be firm and head for the door. Thank them for a stimulating evening, discussion and so on, and bid them goodnight. There's nothing worse than someone who keeps you standing at the door for half an hour while they broach new subjects and take an eternity in saying their goodbyes.

As Shakespeare might have said, 'Tarry not in thy going ... Go!'

> *You don't want to make*
> *people glad twice:*
> *glad to see you come,*
> *and glad to see you go.*
>
> Martha George

IN A NUTSHELL

- To extricate yourself from a lengthy conversation without being insulting, sincerely say, 'I've enjoyed our conversation but unfortunately I have an appointment to keep.' Warmly shake the person's hand and leave.

- If engaged in an emotionally charged conversation, gently touch the other person on the shoulder, express your sincere regrets that you have another commitment, and then leave.

- Be considerate and don't overstay your welcome. YOU must make the first move in taking your leave, not the host.

- Don't prolong your goodbyes.

Saying it all

A friend of mine, Oliver Jorgensen, tells a story that neatly sums up everything laid out in this book. Some years ago, Oliver found himself dining alone at a favourite restaurant when a waiter approached and asked if he would mind if someone else joined him at his table. 'No, that's fine,' he responded, a little put out that a stranger would be encroaching on his personal space.

A LOT IN COMMON

A well-dressed gentleman was ushered over. After a hesitant introduction and a few awkward moments, they broke the ice with some small talk. Amazingly, by the time their meal was served they both realised they had quite a lot in common. And it wasn't long before they found themselves totally absorbed in pleasant conversation as if they'd known each other for years.

The next time Oliver glanced at his watch he couldn't believe that two hours had passed by! As his dining companion had other commitments to attend to, he warmly bade Oliver farewell and thanked him for a marvellous evening. Then he was gone.

What a pleasant evening this turned out to be, Oliver thought, basking in the glow of it all and enjoying another cup of coffee. Then he summoned the waiter for the bill. To his absolute astonishment the waiter said, 'Sir, your account has already been settled by your dining companion.'

This chance evening of pleasant company and conversation with a total stranger remains one of Oliver Jorgensen's fondest memories.

FORMING NEW HABITS

Now that we've addressed the conditioned anxieties and self-imposed limitations that have been holding you back, it's time you make it happen and reap the incredible benefits of friendly conversation for yourself. From this day onwards, practise these principles and techniques with everyone you meet. And before long you'll find yourself being the engaging conversationalist you've always wanted to be. The good thing about this enjoyable journey of discovery is it never ends.

SOME FINAL THOUGHTS ...

In keeping with a theme throughout this book (that is, we learn a lot by listening), you'll have noticed I've used quotes that embody the timeless wisdom of the ages to reflect and reinforce my ideas. And so I'd like to leave you with some fine thought-provoking words, for they encapsulate everything I've shared in this book, and beyond. They come from America's first saint, Elizabeth Ann Seton, and they still ring true today.

> *When so rich a harvest is before us*
> *why do we not gather it?*
> *All is in our hands if we will but use it.*

Elizabeth Ann Seton

About the author

HELPING PEOPLE COMMUNICATE WITH CONFIDENCE!

Renowned author and speaker Laurie Smale grew up thinking he didn't amount to much, let alone have anything meaning-ful to say. So he began listening to others and their stories, believing his journey of tough social circumstance and a poor education was too shameful and insignificant for anyone to be interested in. Yet by stepping into the world of others and soaking in their wisdom, he came to understand that we can all be interesting human beings whatever our situation or station in life. His refreshing approach to speaking effectiveness has helped thousands to believe in themselves and communicate with confidence! His hard-earned ideas and inspirations now form the body of his three-book trilogy and hold the simple secrets on how to make all of this happen – be it effectively conversing with one person or comfortably holding a roomful of people in the palm of your hands!

As with this book, each of these mind-opening publications is a complete entity unto itself yet is especially written to complement the other two books of the trilogy:

BOOK 1. *FINDING ME FINDING YOU*

This book of self-acceptance gets 'You Right First', for true communicating confidence depends on you being comfortable with where you've been, where you're at, and where you'd like to be.

BOOK 2. *HOW TO BE A CONVERSATIONAL SUCCESS! 2ND EDITION*

Now okay with yourself and ready to make the most of who you are, this treasure of a book will open your mind to knowing you have something to say; will show you how to effortlessly strike up a conversation whatever the situation; then deftly guide the interaction to a memorable conclusion.

BOOK 3. *HOW TO TAKE THE PANIC OUT OF PUBLIC SPEAKING 2ND EDITION*

Far from being another boring text book, this final part of the trilogy takes you one incredible step further by showing you how to transfer conversational naturalness up before groups so your listeners connect with you on a human level and believe you're talking to them personally – all *panic free!*

So there you have it, all you need to know about self-worth and communicating effectiveness in one exciting three-book series. So why not cast your fears aside and join those who now communicate with confidence as a direct result of the tried-and-proven ideas and inspirations that await you in these mind-opening books? Be assured they can do the same for you! You can purchase them online from Amazon and other outlets, or from your favourite bookstore, individually or as the author's three-book *Communicate with Confidence!* series.

To contact the author visit:

www.panicfreepublicspeaking.com.au